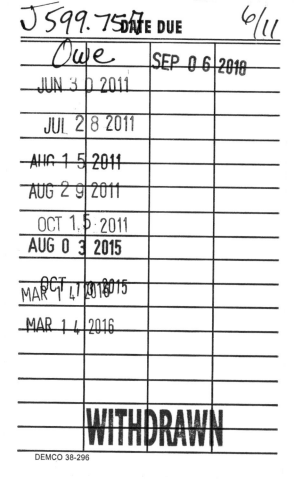

Lion Cubs

by Ruth Owen

Consultants:

Suzy Gazlay, M.A.
Recipient, Presidential Award
for Excellence in Science Teaching

Tricia Holford
Born Free Foundation

BEARPORT
PUBLISHING

New York, New York

Credits

Cover, © Colin Edwards Photography/Shutterstock; 4, © Suzi Eszterhas/Minden Pictures/
FLPA; 5, © Suzi Eszterhas/Minden Pictures/FLPA; 6–7, © Bernd Zoller/Imagebroker/FLPA;
8–9, © ZSSD/Minden Pictures/FLPA; 10–11, © Elliott Neep/FLPA; 12–13, © Paul Sawer/
FLPA; 14, © Dmitriy Kuzmichev/Shutterstock; 15, © Bernd Zoller/Imagebroker/FLPA; 16, ©
Imagebroker/FLPA; 17, © Suzi Eszterhas/Minden Pictures/FLPA; 18, © Suzi Eszterhas/Minden
Pictures/FLPA; 19, © ZSSD/Minden Pictures/FLPA; 20, © Ingo Arndt/Minden Pictures/
FLPA; 21, © Shutterstock; 22T, © Eric Isselée/Shutterstock; 22B, © Antonio Jorge Nunes/
Shutterstock; 23T, © Imagebroker/FLPA; 23B, © Riaan van den Berg/Shutterstock.

Publisher: Kenn Goin
Senior Editor: Lisa Wiseman
Creative Director: Spencer Brinker
Design: Alix Wood
Photo Researcher: Ruby Tuesday Books Ltd

Library of Congress Cataloging-in-Publication Data

Owen, Ruth, 1967-
  Lion cubs / by Ruth Owen.
      p. cm. — (Wild baby animals)
  Includes bibliographical references and index.
  ISBN-13: 978-1-61772-159-5 (library binding)
  ISBN-10: 1-61772-159-X (library binding)
  1. Lion—Infancy—Juvenile literature. I. Title.
  QL737.C23O94 2011
  599.757'139—dc22
                              2010041246

For more information, write to Bearport Publishing Company, Inc., 101 Fifth Avenue,
Suite 6R, New York, New York 10003. Printed in the United States of America in North
Mankato, Minnesota.

121510
10810CGC

10 9 8 7 6 5 4 3 2 1

Contents

Playtime!

Two lion **cubs** play with a big male lion.

The cubs bite him.

The big lion roars, but he doesn't mind the game.

He is the cubs' father.

Lion prides

Lions live in family groups called **prides**.

Each pride usually has one or two males.

A pride also has some females, called lionesses, and their cubs.

The strongest male leads the pride.

He is the father of all the cubs.

Lioness

Cub

Male leader

Lions and lionesses

Adult male lions and lionesses do not look the same.

Adult males are much larger.

They also have long hair on their heads and necks.

The hair is called a mane.

Lion sizes

Male lion

Lioness

Cub

Where do lions live?

Most lions live in Africa.

Some of these lions live in places where there are trees and bushes.

Arctic Ocean

North America

Europe

Asia

Atlantic Ocean

Africa

Pacific Ocean

South America

Indian Ocean

Australia

N
W E
S

Southern Ocean

Antarctica

Where African lions live

Others live on **grasslands**.

Grasslands are dry places with few trees or bushes.

The cubs are born

A lioness gives birth to her cubs in a safe place away from the pride.

She feeds the cubs milk from her body.

She licks the cubs to keep them clean.

Cubs feeding

Lion cubs

The new cubs have spots on their fur.

The spots help them blend into the bushes.

This makes it hard for enemies to see the cubs.

When the cubs are four weeks old, their mother brings them to meet the pride.

What do lions eat?

Lions eat other animals, such as zebras.

Cubs start to eat meat when they are six weeks old.

They still drink their mother's milk, though.

Six-week-old cubs feeding

Learning to hunt

Lionesses do most of the hunting for the pride.

Cubs learn to hunt by watching their mother attack **prey**.

They practice hunting by attacking her tail.

They also practice by chasing and attacking one another.

Growing up

Most females stay with the pride for all of their lives.

Males leave the pride when they are three years old.

They go to live in groups with other males.

Someday, they will be leaders of their own prides!

Young females

Young male lion

21

Glossary

cubs (KUHBZ) the babies of some animals, such as lions, bears, and tigers

grasslands (GRASS-landz) hot, dry places with a lot of grass and small plants; only a few trees and bushes grow there

prey (PRAY) animals that are hunted by other animals for food; zebras and large antelopes, called wildebeests, are the prey of lions

Prey

prides (PRIDEZ) groups of lions; many of the lions in a pride are related

Index

Read more

Landau, Elaine. *Big Cats: Hunters of the Night (Animals After Dark).* Berkeley Heights, NJ: Enslow (2008).

Orme, Helen. *Lions in Danger (Wildlife Survival).* New York: Bearport (2007).

Squire, Ann O. *Lions (A True Book).* New York: Children's Press (2005).

Walker, Sarah. *Big Cats (Eye Wonder).* New York: DK Publishing (2002).

Learn more online

To learn more about lions, visit **www.bearportpublishing.com/WildBabyAnimals**

About the author

Ruth Owen has been developing, editing, and writing children's books for more than ten years. She lives in Cornwall, England, just minutes from the ocean. Ruth loves gardening and caring for her family of llamas.